Richard was educated by the
University of Life, at Rock Bottom.
He undertook a crash course on survival,
he achieved a 10/10 pass.

First published in 1996 by cantecia
21 Grafton Underwood
NN14 3AB

ISBN 0 9528198 0 5

Cover design by Richard Wilkins
Printed by Candor Print, Northampton.

DEDICATION

To the Universal power of love
that held me, whilst I held the pen.

for James happy birthday '96.
it can only get better x

INTRODUCTION

If you accept, as I do, that love is a real energy
then this book you are holding
is far more than just a book.

I do not believe in luck, fate and co-incidences.
Therefore you and this book were meant to meet..

Enjoy your new friend.

Richard

Words are like maps...
...both can show you the way.

The difference between having
a 1 out of 10 life
and a 10 out of 10 life
is a choice...

Happiness is an inside job!

Trust is an act of faith
that doubt hadn't the courage to believe in.

The greatest superstition
is believing that more is better.

Tragedy is opportunity for change...

Nothing ends
it only changes.

Pain's love is fear
Pain's fear is love.

The inability to trust
will keep many a door closed in your life
but then why should you believe me?...

Not to acknowledge your own greatness
will simply deny it the right to exist.

A million tears have been shed,
for what people thought but never said.

Disappointments are born of expectations...

To believe it - is ok
to know it - is better
to apply it - is best.

If you had to carry what you wanted
would you still want it?

Try pulling that door instead of pushing
you may get a surprise!

Anger is merely the absence of love.

Whilst it is a truly wondrous walk
along this pathway we call life
there is nothing to stop us
laying paving slabs of our own...

When you place a condition on happiness
you create a potential for pain.

We kid ourselves it's working
when we know full well it's not,
so we put a comma
where we ought to put a dot.

Wishes are ok - but intentions are for real.

I know of a place where love, hope, forgiveness and so much more can be found...
...it's called a mirror.

Bitterness is an illness which is unique to man.

Your mind is a garden for your thoughts

If you plant flowers,
you will get flowers.

If you plant potatoes,
you will get potatoes.

If you plant nothing,
you will get weeds.

Time is the Universal currency.

Why do so many find it easier
to blame themselves for a wrong
than to credit themselves for a right?

When anger is greeted with anger,
the result can only be more anger.

What is the difference between
pretending to be happy
and being happy?

Fears have no place in the now
they can only exist in the future,
yet when we arrive in the future
it simply becomes the now.
Fears have no place in the now...

Laughter is the Universal language.

You are the cause of your life
not the effect of it.

Nothing in life is how it is
For how it is, is simply how you see it.

If health was everything
all healthy people would be happy.

You can be happy with money
but money won't make you happy.

All the difference
will not make the way you think...
...yet the way you think
will make all the difference.

The very bottom line is..
...there is no bottom line.

Pain is like a sculptors chisel:
it chips away at the shapeless block of stone
to reveal the masterpiece
which is hidden within.

Everything, but everything other than love is on loan.

Comparisons create winners and losers.

If you pursue what hurts you...

...then it will hurt you.

Your health is physical manifestation
of your thoughts,
so make them good!

Leopards can't change their spots
any more than chameleons
can change their colour!

Backward thinking people use their thoughts
to **examine** their lives
Forward thinking people use their thoughts
to **create** their lives.

No person is harder on us
than we are on ourselves.

I once became a grown up
but that was only overnight,
then I looked around and saw
the kids had got it right.

You must gaze through acceptance
before you can see perfection.

A habit is having the will power not to stop.

True friendship is unrecognisable
when concealed behind a mask
of happiness and well being.
It is only when tragedy strikes
that the true face of friendship
will become recognisable.

The foundations of your future
are the memories of your past,
if you only use the best ones
the house you build will last.

.

Appreciation is often realised too late
to be appreciated by those
we meant to appreciate.

Grief is an emotion experienced solely by the living.

All truly great people are known
for what they gave
not what they got.

Communication is like the thread which runs through a pearl necklace, it is not noticeable, yet without it everything would fall apart.

Actions follow thoughts
thoughts follow nothing.

Change **is** that second chance...

Probabilities are merely possibilities
with odds placed on them.
Possibilities do not have odds
they are unlimited.

Your thoughts create your actions
you create your thoughts.

A lifetime of good fortune
cannot make of the person
what tragedy can in a single day.

Being unhappy
requires considerably more effort
than being happy.

Stepping back isn't stepping off!

See money as an object
not an objective.

The greatest place to which you can travel
is the hearts of the needy.

Remember, bad times go away
when you don't see them as bad times.

Your physical is the bow.
Your spirit the arrow,
pain the pulling back of the bow.
So it is: the further back the bow is pulled
the further the arrow will fly.

It is said that it is best to turn
and face the enemy...
...surely it is better
to have no enemy to face.

If you've taken for granted
you've taken too much.

In most cases the difference between
a **do** and a **don't**
is a **doubt**.

Ripples will continue to cross the pool
long after the stone has been cast.

Happiness can never be taken away,
only given away.

Bitterness is far more visible
than most people realise.
Be warned! It is also very unattractive.

Love is a state of being...
...not being in a state.

Doubt does to progress,
what a brake does to a wheel.

How can anything be too late
when our lives are surrounded by eternity?

What rain does for the flower...
...tears do for the soul.

Stress can't cope with calmness!

Trying to find happiness is like
a dog trying to catch it's own tail...
...so why chase after
what you have already got?

Calmness is the key
which will open all doors.

Photographs are records of the past,
only the best ones go in the album.
Treat your memories the same.

How would you feel about someone
who criticises you
as much as you criticise yourself?

Happiness is a free option
with every life!

We can't always control
the things that affect us,
but we **can** control
the affect they have on us.

The past doesn't equal the future
it creates habits.

Everything is created
first in our imagination,
if it were not, how would we know
what it was we wanted?

People may hand you the bullets
but you don't have to use the gun.

'Never' knows no compromise
and much regret.

A relationship is like a glass of wine,
unless you put back what you have taken out,
it will run dry.

Since birth you will have endured thousands, probably millions of troublesome situations, how many of them affect you today?

Birds carry no baggage
and they can fly.

Hindsight is a wonderful thing
it also means it's a bit late.

True faith works
as well on Monday in the bathroom
as it does on Sunday at Church.

Excessive strength is often
a cover up for weakness.

Your past exists in your memory alone.
Your memories are pure thought.
You can change your thoughts,
so it is that the past can be changed.

To learn from a mistake - is a lesson
not to learn from a mistake - is a mistake!

Don't get stuck with problems
go on ahead of them -
they rarely take the trouble to catch you up.

Those who look to another
will find another,
Those who look to themselves
will find themselves.

Look what you can get rid of
not more of...

So many people would be grateful
if you could spare them
just a little of your time.
So never wish it away.

It is impossible to have an argument
unless you consent to it.

Trust is an investment in the invisible.

In death I see much beauty
although my view's not widely shared,
so for the only thing that's guaranteed
so few will be prepared.

Blaming oneself can be far more destructive than blaming others ...they can walk away.

You must see the world as a wonderful place
before it can be one.

Contentment cannot be found outside us -
yet it is where so many
continue to look for it...

Hope is a most wonderful thing,
never insult it by calling it false...

There are no disabled
...only less abled.

If it works, accept it:
Would you dismantle a clock
which keeps perfect time
simply to find out why
it keeps perfect time?

Jealousy is insecurity
in fancy dress.

I'd been searching for the answers
now I see the answer is just a part.
The secret is in the question,
it's where all answers start.

Knowledge absorbed is knowledge.
Knowledge applied is wisdom.

Blaming others for the way your life
is going, is like getting on a train
going in the wrong direction
and then blaming the train.

The saddest tear is the one you cannot cry.

You can't do better than your best
with the grade of best
you've past the test.

Losing a temper is a good thing,
who wants one anyway?

Boredom is simply lack of imagination.

Act differently towards others
if you want them to act
differently towards you.

Stress is the way you act
not what you attract.

Trying to live up to others expectations
is like you wearing their clothes
...they wouldn't fit
and the colours wouldn't suit you.

Assumption is a free gift to all.
Never waste it by assuming the worst
when the best is always an option.

Remember - they are doing their best.

It's just as well for us
that inventors of the past
didn't adopt the theory
that they had to see it first!

Many a tear is born of haste.

It is often better to have lost than not,
for it is when we go in search
of what we have lost that we may find
something even greater.

Kindness is a sunbeam that
pierces the darkest memory.

Discontentment is when reality
is no match for the imagination.

Man does not damage the environment,
only ignorance can do that.

Unhappiness is a resistance
to a change of belief.

You can try to be better than others
or help others better themselves.

When we choose to think
about something we are against,
it creates a blockage inside us,
this is pain.
When we choose to think
about what we are for,
it creates a flow inside us,
this is joy.

Self worth is the level of love
you consider yourself worthy of -
the more you value yourself
the more love you'll get.

Reach down to those
who can't reach up to you.

All great change will be met by resistance.
It is not the change that is the problem,
anyone can change.
It is the resistance to change
that is the problem.
Resistance is a belief
and a belief can be changed.

Revenge is a need for pain.

Have you ever stopped to wonder
just how much we take for granted?
So don't forget to water the seed
after it has been planted.

Don't look for the light to show the way,
become the light and **be** the way.

Loneliness is the most common
illness in the world
it is also the least understood.

Hatred doesn't come naturally -
it has to be taught.

People who don't judge
don't forgive -
they don't need to.

The reason I am happy is because
I don't like the alternatives...

Time is a most valuable commodity,
invest it well and it will show
you a good return long after
you've passed the need for a pension.

There are those who see things
as someone else's fault.
There are those who see things
as their own fault.
And there are those
who don't see fault.

There is a beginning within every ending...

The secret to having a happy life
is knowing that there is no secret
to having a happy life!

If you owe ten million
or if you owe ten pounds,
if you haven't got it
they are merely different sounds.

Encouragement does to people
what hot air does to the balloon.

There is a time to love,
there is a time to grieve,
there is a time to stay,
and there is a time to leave.

Watch out for possessions -
they can turn into obsessions.

Looking at a problem
when you feel depressed
is like looking at a money spider
through a microscope.

Guilt is the self denial of forgiveness
which we impose upon ourselves
and by that token
the sworn enemy of progress.

If you doubt a thought
is a real thing -
wiggle your thumb!

If you have a problem
try to make it a positive one
but be careful not to make it too positive
or it won't be a problem!

Mankind is like a herd of buffalo.
It all seems like total chaos -
but if you rise high above you will see
they are all moving in the same direction.

We can only experience anything
with our thoughts.
We are now beginning to understand
this simple truth.
With this understanding
we will come to know
that all we ever wanted
we already have.

The teaching may come from others
but the learning must come from **you**.

ACKNOWLEDGMENTS

Alf and Shirley
for encouraging me from the start.

Ann and Graham
for your encouragement and help with funding my leaflets

Anthea Meakins
who introduced me to myself

Ann Milne
who gives me more support than Man. United get in a season!

Barry Dove
who provided me with friendship when I needed it.

Bill and Irene
who opened the doors of their home for my very first talk.

Carol Abbott
*for allowing my work - through yourself and your shop
- to reach so many people.*

Chris and Erika
who gave me love.

Dr Bernie Siegal
a heaven sent messenger of hope.

Dr Wayne Dyer
whose work is a lesson to us all.

Gordon and Mo
*patients from the Cynthia Spencer hospice
who both taught me about the power of giving.*

Ivor and Marge
two stars that shine brightly.

Jack Pogson
for believing in me enough to fund the first run of 'Being 10/10'.

Jackie and Deryk
who listened when I needed to talk.

Jane Pentland
who, through her death taught me so much about living.

Janet and Richard
whose work is a light for me to follow.

Joy Agar
who saw the potential of my work before I did.

Joy Earl
who broke my fall to Rock Bottom.

Joyce
who worked with me before Rock Bottom and with me on Rock Bottom.

Mark Carr
my friend who carried me when I couldn't carry myself.

Mel
*who watches from paradise
and whose enthusiasm proved stronger than life itself.*

Mo
who gave me the key to her home, when I had no home.

Mum Bell
for being a constant river of love and support in everything I do.

My Sister Doreen
whose zest for life is an example for me to follow.

My Sister Did
who kept my phone ringing when I was on Rock Bottom.

My Brother John
who taught me there are no problems, only situations.

Steff and Cathy
for the loan of a roof - and more.

Steve Pentland
who dared to believe in me when others didn't.

Sue and Tony Kelly
who gave me their friendship and lent me their home.

Wendy Wilkins
whose love and kindness allowed me extra years with my Dad.

—————— // ——————

My Mum and Dad
*who I know are proud and watch over me
from where they live in paradise.*

My children
Carl, Lee and Oliver
who have always been and will always be my teachers.

Gillian, my Wife
my teacher, student, partner and lover.